# Contents

# Characters

**POP:** Dan's old uncle. He's a bit of a know-all about fishing.

**DAN:** A lad with many girl-friends. He takes each one fishing to find out which one is really for him!

# DON'T TRY THIS AT HOME

By John Townsend

Series Editors: Steve Barlow and Steve Skidmore

Published by Heinemann Educational Publishers
Halley Court, Jordan Hill, Oxford OX2 8EJ
A division of Reed Educational and Professional Publishing Ltd

OXFORD MELBOURNE AUCKLAND
JOHANNESBURG BLANTYRE GABORONE
IBADAN PORTSMOUTH (NH) USA CHICAGO

First published 2002

06 05 04 03 02
10 9 8 7 6 5 4 3 2 1

ISBN 0 435 21384 9

Illustrations by Pete Smith
Cover design by Shireen Nathoo Design
Designed and typeset by Artistix, Thame, Oxon
Printed and bound in Great Britain by Biddles Ltd

Tel: 01865 888058  www.heinemann.co.uk

**MEL:** One of Dan's girl-friends. She is fed up at being on the river bank all night.

**DI:** Another of Dan's girl-friends. She isn't happy with fishing all night. She is very moody.

**SUE:** Dan's third girl-friend. She is much more fun and gives both Dan and Pop a run for their money!

# SCENE ONE

Pop, Dan and Mel are sitting on the river bank. Pop and Dan are fishing. Mel is fed up. It is getting dark. They have a few bags and fishing tackle with them.

**DAN:**      This is the life.

**POP:**      Ssh.

**DAN:** It's nice here.

**POP:** Ssh.

**DAN:** And quiet. *(Pause)* Dead quiet.

**POP:** Ssh.

**MEL:** I'm cold.

**DAN:** It's a great bit of river just here.

**MEL:** Chilly.

**POP:** Ssh.

**DAN:** I love it.

**MEL:** I don't. It's damp.

**POP:** Ssh.

**DAN:** Uncle Pop?

**POP:** Ssh. What?

**DAN:** Why do you keep saying that?

**POP:** What?

**DAN:** You keep saying 'Ssh'.

**POP:** You have to keep quiet.

**MEL:** How boring.

**POP:** Noise will scare the fish.

**MEL:** I want to go home.

**POP:** You can't have fun like this at home.

| | |
|---|---|
| **MEL:** | Fun? I hate this. |
| **DAN:** | You wanted to come. |
| **MEL:** | I didn't. |
| **DAN:** | You did. I said, 'Do you want to come out with me?' You said 'yes'. |
| **MEL:** | I thought you'd take me to a good place. Like a disco. Like the cinema. |
| **POP:** | See this hook? It can take your eye out. You must beware when I cast the line. |
| **MEL:** | Try telling the maggot that. |
| **POP:** | Never try this at home. |
| **DAN:** | I told you Pop knew a lot, didn't I? |
| **MEL:** | Dan, when a boy asks me out, I don't want to sit all night with HIS OLD UNCLE! |
| **POP:** | Sssssh! |

**DAN:** I always go fishing with Uncle Pop. I told you we were going fishing.

**MEL:** No. You said we could go out for some good fish. I had other things in mind.

**DAN:** What did you have in mind?

**MEL:** A hot plate of cod and chips. With mushy peas and ketchup! I'm starving.

**DAN:** Pop's got some food in his bag.

**MEL:** I bet there's no hot dog with onions.

**DAN:** No. Ham rolls with jam.

**MEL:** Yuk!

**DAN:** Pop, we'd like a bite.

**POP:** Maybe soon if you hold the rod still.

**MEL:** Not that sort of bite. I mean real food.

**POP:** Help yourself. Have a look in my bag. Don't make a noise. Fish can hear us.

**DAN:** *(Looking into a big bag)* What's in the tubs, Pop?

**POP:** Rice pud. I put in a nip of rum, too. And there's a pot of jam to mix with it.

**MEL:** No thanks.

**DAN:** What's in these pots, Pop? I can't see.

**POP:** Cold custard. Nice.

**MEL:** Yuk! Dan, why can't you take me to see a film like any normal lad?

**POP:** Ssh.

**DAN:** I only like films about fishing.

**POP:** 'Jaws' is a good film. There was a fish in that. Pass me that tub of rice pud.

**DAN:** Okay, Pop. I'll stir it for you. I can't see very well. Here you are. Funny smell.

**POP:** Nice. You can't beat a spot of jam and rice pud. *(He starts to eat)*

**MEL:** I'll stick with ham rolls. *(She eats)*

**DAN:** So it looks like custard for me.

*(They sit in silence, all eating.)*

**POP:** This is the life.

**MEL:** It's boring. I'd rather watch paint dry. I'd rather eat slugs in garlic jelly.

**DAN:** We can do that tomorrow night!

**POP:** Ssh. I think I got a twitch.

**MEL:** You'd better take a tablet.

**DAN:** He means on the line. This could be it!

**POP:** Quick! Pass me more bait.

**DAN:** *(Head in the bag)* I can't find the bait.

**POP:** Come on, lad. I need more bait. Hurry! *(He stands and tugs on the rod)*

**DAN:** It's no good, Pop. I can't find it.

**POP:** Quick. Pass that tub. I've got a tug!

**DAN:** This tub is full of rice pud.

**POP:** Don't talk daft. I've eaten it. Hurry and pass me the tub of maggots.

*(Dan stares. Mel falls about laughing.)*

**DAN:** Urgh!! I feel sick! Don't you see what you've done?

**MEL:** What a great night out! This is so funny. Uncle Pop ate a tub of maggots with jam!

**POP:** *(Suddenly going mad and shouting)* And now the fish has got away!

**MEL:** Well, you know why, don't you?

**POP:** WHAT DO YOU KNOW ABOUT FISHING?!!

**MEL:** Try this for a tip. When you're on a river bank … don't eat maggots and shout!

**DAN:** SHSH SHSH SHSH SHSH SHSH SHSH!

**MEL:** And please … DON'T TRY THIS AT HOME!

# SCENE TWO

> The next evening. Pop, Dan and Di are sitting on the river bank. Pop and Dan are fishing. Di is fed up. It is getting dark. They have bags and fishing tackle.

**DAN:**        This is the life.

**POP:**        *(Sniffs)*

**DAN:**     It's nice here.

**POP:**     (Sniffs)

**DAN:**     And quiet. (Pause) Dead quiet.

**POP:**     (Sniffs)

**DI:**     I'm cold.

**POP:**     (Sniffs)

**DAN:**     I love it.

**DI:**     I don't. It's damp.

**DAN:**     Pop?

**POP:**     (Sniffs) What?

**DAN:**     Why do you keep doing that?

**POP:**     What?

**DAN:**     You keep sniffing.

**POP:**     I've got a cold.

**DI:**     That's because it's so cold and damp.

**POP:**  This fresh air is good for you. *(Sniffs)*

**DI:**  Dan, why has HE come with us?

**DAN:**  Uncle Pop always comes fishing.

**DI:**  You asked me out for a meal. Not this!

**POP:**  I've got lots of Cuppa Soups in the car. We'll have a brew-up soon. I've got more brown ale in the boot.

**DAN:**  There you are, Di. A nice meal out.

**DI:**  I thought we'd go out to a pub. Or for a curry. A candle-lit dinner for two.

**DAN:**  Really? What for?

**POP:**  You can't beat fishing. *(Sneezes)*

**DI:**  He's got a cold. It's from sitting on a damp river bank. Did you hear a plop? Was it a fish?

**DAN:**  Yeh! Pop, did you hear it? Is it a bite?

**POP:** It was me.

**DAN:** You?

**POP:** My teef!

**DI:** His what?

**DAN:** Your what?

**POP:** My teef!

**DAN:** Your teef?

| | |
|---|---|
| **DI:** | He means his TEETH! His false teeth! They shot into the river when he sneezed! |
| **POP:** | Quick! Pass a rod. I'll fish them out! |
| **DAN:** | Here you are, Uncle Pop. You can do it! |
| **DI:** | Does he know what he's doing? |
| **DAN:** | Just watch. He knows what to do. He'll get them back. It's all skill. |
| **DI:** | Are you sure? |
| **POP:** | I've got it! I've got a bite! |
| **DI:** | A bite from his own teeth! |
| **POP:** | It's skill. But I must warn you, Di. Never use a rod like this yourself. |
| **DI:** | Wow! Thanks for the warning! |
| **POP:** | Never forget. Don't try this at home. |
| **DAN:** | Look! You've got them. You got a bite. |

**DI:** Very clever.

**POP:** *(He takes the teeth off the hook and puts them in his mouth)* That's better. Now I can eat my grub.

**DI:** He just put those teeth in his mouth! They've been in that filthy river.

**POP:** That's not all. There was a worm on the hook. Now it's got under my plate.

**DI:** Yuk! I feel sick.

**POP:** Hold on … these teeth aren't mine! I got the wrong ones. Never mind, they'll do. I'll get some food from the car. *(He goes)*

**DI:** Your uncle makes me feel sick. That river's so dirty. No wonder you haven't got any fish yet. I bet they're all dead.

**DAN:** No, it's full of life. Look just down in the reeds. There's lots of frog-spawn. That's a sign of a good river.

**DI:** Frog-spawn? My brother wants some for his pond. He likes tadpoles and frogs.

**DAN:** You could take some back for him.

**DI:** I'm not going near it. It's all slimy.

**DAN:** You don't have to touch it. Just scoop it up. Here's an empty bottle. I'll put some in here. It's just like jelly. *(He fills a beer bottle with brown water)*

**DI:**  Be careful. Don't fall in.

**DAN:**  Like Pop says: 'Don't try this at home'. Here you are. It's full of muddy water, frog-spawn and even a few tadpoles.

**DI:**  Yuk! I'll put it in the bag.

**DAN:**  You can come again tomorrow if you like.

**DI:**  I'd rather lie on a bed of nails with my eyes pulled out by a mad axe man.

**DAN:** Really? I'd far rather go fishing.

**POP:** *(Enters with bags and sniffing)* Cuppa Soups! Hot water in the flask. *(Dan and Di make the soup)* Ah! Good. There's a bottle of beer left in my bag.

**DI:** Ooer! What's Pop doing?

**POP:** Just the job. *(He swigs)* Mmm, this brown ale is frothy. Nice. *(He knocks back the bottle with a growl)*

**DI:** What's wrong with your uncle?

**DAN:** Just a frog in his throat. Oh heck! Look what he's done! Now his teeth have shot out again.

**DI:** Does he often roll in the mud like that?

**DAN:** He drank all the frog-spawn! Let me give you a tip. Whatever you do …

**BOTH:** DON'T TRY THIS AT HOME!

# S CENE  T HREE

*The next evening on the river bank. Pop and Dan are fishing. Sue is frying with a pan on a gas-ring. It is getting dark. They have a few bags and a bucket.*

**DAN:**       This is the life.

**POP:**       Mmm.

**DAN:**       It's nice here.

**POP:** Mmm.

**DAN:** And quiet. *(Pause)* Dead quiet.

**POP:** Mmm.

**SUE:** I'm cold.

**POP:** Mmm.

**DAN:** Peace and quiet. Just the job.

**SUE:** Very chilly.

**DAN:** It's a great bit of river just here.

**SUE:** Damp. So I'll put on a coat. Fine!

**DAN:** Pop?

**POP:** Mmm. What?

**DAN:** Why do you keep saying that?

**POP:** What?

**DAN:** You keep saying 'Mmm'.

**POP:** I'm thinking. That's all. And waiting.

**SUE:** What are you waiting for, Uncle Pop?

**POP:** I'm waiting for you to moan.

**SUE:** What about?

**POP:** The cold and the damp and the mud.

**SUE:** No – I love it.

**POP:** You've got a good one here, Dan!

**SUE:** You can't beat the outdoor life. When Dan asked me out I wasn't so sure.

**DAN:** Why not?

**SUE:** It was your chat-up line. You said, 'Will you come out with me to catch something?' I thought it might be the flu!

**DAN:** I asked you out to the bank.

**SUE:** I thought you meant the Nat West in the High Street! But the *river* bank is another kettle of fish. Talking of fish …

**POP:** You can't rush. Never hurry a fish.

**SUE:** Do you ever catch any?

**POP:** Over the years I've caught about … one.

**SUE:** One?

**DAN:** But it got away.

**SUE:** Only one fish? In all those years? Was it a trout?

**DAN:** No. A tuna fish.

**SUE:** A tuna fish? They don't live in rivers!

**POP:** This one did. It was in a sandwich. It fell from a boat. Very nice with onion.

**SUE:** You're telling fibs! I tried to catch a whale once. I went ice-fishing. I cut a hole in the ice and waited.

**DAN:** What happened?

**SUE:** A loud voice filled the night.

**POP:** What did it say?

**SUE:** It said, 'Don't go under the ice.'

**POP:** Maybe it was the voice of God.

**SUE:** No. It was the boss of the ice rink!

**DAN:** Very funny! Hey, those chips smell good.

**SUE:** All I need now are fish. The pan's hot.

**POP:** There's a crate of beer in the car.

**SUE:** Then I'll go and get it. Pass the keys. I'll catch you a fish when I get back. I bet I'll get the first bite. *(She goes)*

**POP:** She's a fine lass. You've got a winner this time. I like her. She's the one for you!

**DAN:** If she wins the bet you'll look a fool.

**POP:** Ssh! Look down here in the net. It's a big eel I got earlier. I've already won!

**DAN:** Great! Don't let it get away.

**POP:** Don't worry. I'll put it in this bucket. *(He gets a bucket and scoops up the eel)* It's got big teeth as well. It can give a nasty bite. Ssh, here she comes.

**SUE:** *(Enters)* One crate of beer. Still no fish? I'll show you how to get a bite. I bet you a fiver I'll get the first catch.

**POP:** Done. *(He winks at Dan)*

**SUE:** Right. Here goes … *(She casts a line)*

**POP:** If you catch a salmon, you get my car!

**DAN:** With a year's tax and petrol.

**SUE:** Get ready to hand over the keys. I've got a bite. It's big. Help me pull it in!

**DAN:** *(He grabs the rod)* Wow, I see what you mean. Give us a hand, Uncle Pop.

**POP:** *(He also grabs hold)* Slowly does it. Here it comes. This is a beauty …

*(They all stare as they pull out a Tesco trolley with a tin of salmon in it.)*

**SUE:** I've won! A tin of salmon in a trolley! Has anyone got a tin opener?

**POP:** I don't believe it! Let me get it up on the bank. One … two … three … Aah! Ow! *(He falls back onto the frying-pan)* I've got hot fat in my lap. Aaah!

**SUE:** I'll get some cold water. Undo your belt. This will cool you down. *(She tips the bucket in his trousers)*

**DAN:** Oh heck! The eel! In his pants!

*(Pop jumps to his feet and leaps about – like an Irish jig!)*

**DAN:** I've never seen him dance before.

**SUE:** It's an Irish jig. River Dance!

*(Dan points to the audience.)*

**DAN:** There's a crowd looking.

**SUE:** Then we'd better tell them.

**DAN:** Tell them what?

**SUE:** *(Shouts)* A word of warning to you all …

**DAN:** Please … whatever you do….

**ALL:** DON'T TRY THIS AT HOME!